1

GUNS

Locked in the cabinet
with all of the guns

Do all sons kill their fathers
or all fathers kill their sons?

I can feel the vibrations
I can hear the drill

I've locked myself
Here

TASTE

Guns taste bad, but people still eat them,
in the pursuit of happiness and more often
freedom

BAD

Sing into my skull
Whistle past my ears

Tell me again how to lie

Be a semblance of true

Because this gun is for hire

Guns

Taste

Bad

Landon Chapman

Copyright
Identifier-ISBN (Hardback) 9781737930723
2021 Guns Taste Bad Landon Chapman
All Rights Reserved

Copyright © 2021/2022 by Landon Chapman
Guns Taste Bad All rights reserved. No part of this publication may be reproduced, distributed, or transmitted in any form or by any means, including photocopying, recording, or other electronic or mechanical methods, without the prior written permission of the publisher, except in the case of brief quotations embodied in critical reviews and certain other noncommercial uses permitted by copyright law.

For permission requests, write to the publisher, addressed:

Attention: Permissions Coordinator
Mango Jane Publishing
Mango Jane Books *Imprint*
P.O. Box 231781
Encinitas, CA 92023

MangoJane.Co

Quantity sales: Special discounts are available on quantity purchases by corporations, associations, and others. For details, contact the publisher address or e-mail.

Dedicated to
Spenser

Featuring *Odysseus* poem selected
for FALL LINES publication by
The Jasper Project

PRAISE FOR

Guns Taste Bad:

"Landon Chapman is an emerging new American Poet that writes from the soul. Flashes of cold winter nights, hard truths and broken hearts will take you down a road rising within the power of words, poetry and observations about the human existence."

-Machel Shull, Author of *Spiritual*

"Chapman's poetry is raw and real, reminding us that death is a familiar stranger on a subway waiting to greet us."

-Tracy G. Howard, editor and poet

GUNS: Post Masculinity

21	The Tall Mirror That Belittles
22	Prodigal Son Blues
23	Odysseus: Your Old Man
25	We Are Not What Our Fathers Make Us
26	The Appended Self
28	Boon Ruin
29	Last Night
31	It Ain't About the Wand
32	Party Girls Feel Nothing
34	Vera
36	Today I Felt My Menace
38	Well, She'll Lead 'Em On
40	Black Ringed Eye
41	Gone is the Cash
42	Pugilist
44	Wallop Festival Scarecrow
45	Body Grapple Shindig
46	Jazz Hands
47	Don't Make Us Jam You UP
48	Acceptable Losses

49	I Loved You in the Morning
50	Displacement
52	Sesame Street Drug Test Blues
54	Down in Tijuana
55	Outlawyers
56	Twelve Year Olds Don't Know About Watergate
58	It's Hard to Live in the City
60	You're Gunna Carry That Weight

TASTE: Introspection

65	Guns Taste Bad
67	Adam Kadman and the Folks Who Eat Him
68	The Ziggurat of Self Appraisal
69	Hecate
71	Diogenes
72	Diogenes II: Spittoon
74	The Hand That Offends
76	Smashed Thumbs
77	Plantation Wedding
79	Practicin' Haptics Physically
81	Heavyweight Round 12
82	Appaloosa
84	Reprieve
85	Loam Sleep
86	You Creatures
87	Animal Shame
89	I Seen Animals
90	It Could Have Been Well Designed
91	Freeloaders
92	A Ball of Mental Illness

93	Corporate Adjacent
95	The Vault Opens
97	You Gave Me Acid
98	Well I'm Not Sure If I'm Back
99	I Have Killed
100	A Greasy Spot on the Heart

BAD: Estrangement

105	You've Got a Face With a View
106	Upchucked
108	She's So Tall
109	You Were a Library
110	When You Were Leaving
112	Doubt
113	Thanks Mom
115	Long Distance Tokyo
117	It's Nice You're So Happy
118	Come Back Soon
120	The Hardest Part of Being a Broken Family
121	Bonghwang
122	I've Seen You in the Wind
123	Headlights Out
124	Shame Rain on Me
126	Medusa
128	Slipping Tongues
129	Soviet Moonshine
131	Obduracy

- 133   The Hole in the Pipe Your Ex Gave You
- 134   Nairobi 98
- 135   Your Sunflower Dress
- 137   The Factory is Closing
- 138   Boober in the Land of Ferrofluid
- 139   Blue Little Bell
- 141   Metatron
- 145   About the Author

FOREWORD

Chapman grew up in a northern town and currently lives in the deep south where he longs for a taste of cold winters and golden summers. Chapman is a prolific poet who enjoys pipe smoking, drinking and speaking more than his fair share.

In *Guns Taste Bad,* Chapman gives us three segments of poetry. First in *Guns*, he explores what it is to be a man in a post masculine world. Then in *Taste,* he turns inward for soulful introspection. Finally, in *Bad,* he delves into the personal sorrows of the postmodern experience.

Chapman's poetry is raw and real, reminding us that death is a familiar stranger on the subway waiting to greet us. Loss permeates his poetry with a soulful melancholy.

Chapman attended five different high schools and traveled between continents, straddling a family divided. Chapman lived abroad in Singapore. His journeys to Asia gave him a deeper grasp of connections between people and culture.

He spent three years at Lander University studying writing and history. Currently he is working on his first novel.

Chapman has loved and lost. His poetry challenges you to listen and perceive.

Guns taste bad. Enjoy.

Tracy Howard, Editor

Guns

The Tall Mirror Belittles

The smell of dandelions reminds me of your
Kisses

Of how they were so small
And sweet

Of how small I painted your feelings

I had to look down to you

You were Short
Like your hair

Like my temper

But I looked down on your problems

And from where I stood

High on my icy white tower

I saw no mountains
No hardship

But now
Brought low to the dirt and rocks

What might not have been mountains
Are still impassable hills

And the only thing looming high above
them

Was my tower

Icy

And wight

Prodigal Son Blues

Father away
I have moved from you

In distance
In kind

In semblance
In mind

Farther
My spirit I command

This son that I was

That man that you were

Now we are neither

Both forsaken
Both forsook

Father
Into my hands
A violence has took

My soul I command
Farther

Who dished it out better?
Who took the most hits?

Hard to say

Understand

Farther
Into your hands

Odysseus: Your Old Man

Kid ask your mom
When I can see you again

It's been a while
Seen you grown

In pictures
Glowing and far

These states are oceans
These debts the whole of space

Think I'm a caveman

But I got a job
And the monies on the way

Tell your mom
The monies comin'

Seen you grew out your hair kid
Hope schools goin' well

I know it's been some time
But if these states are oceans

I'm a sailor

If these debts are space

Kid I'm an astronaut

I'd sail these angry waves
I'll traverse this silent void

Hey kid ask your mom
When I can see you again

Money's a comin'
N' so am I

We Are What Our Fathers Make Us

Once this blade is unsheathed
And some other uncompromising shtick

Real cool
Old school

Masculine
Or what it was supposed to be

Not the one that makes life
But a real strong proxy

Losing the coin toss

We all start out the same
That is 'til some of us grow balls

N' ifin' we can't create life
What's the flip side of that coin

Uncompromising
Not as a compliment

But as hormones
Or that specific

Ignition switch

Testosterone

Wants us to be

Toxic
Antiseptic
Sterile

The Appended Self

Now
Locked in the cabinet
With all of the guns

Do all sons kill their fathers?

Or do all fathers kill their sons?

I can feel the vibrations
I can hear the drill

I've locked myself

Here
In the safe
Away from your will

But the bit bores on in

Soon you'll scrape through

However thick the barrier

There is no adieu

So you'll burrow back into me
Lay your eggs in my skull

Crack my sternum apart
Again crawl into my soul

You're the twisting screw
Beneath my thumb nail

I'd pull you out if I could
But I've set this ship to sail

The snapping of wood

Sawdust in my mouth

Hello

Boon Ruin

You wanted to travel with him

Protect what he saw and heard

But you know even Jesus was betrayed
By a friend for some loot

And it terrifies you by your soul and beard

That you're his Judas
That you're his end

You can't shake the feeling this damnable fate

All you can do is be there
All you can do is hope

But it's there, around your neck this weight.

His footprints in the sand
You're careful not to tread

These holy instances of friendship

You see them blurring
You see them destroyed

You are the anchor of a slowly sinking ship

But Jesus was a sailor
And he walked upon the water

How does the salt taste?
My friend,

Peter?

Last Night

Looking for a higher being

I took to potencies

I fell into my bed
With Pupils wider than my eyes

Golgotha surrounded me
The three monuments stabbed into the air

I crawled up his naked body
I tore hair from his beard

I bit off fingers
I pushed thumbs through eyes

Reached in through the spear hole
Pulled his guts out

Drank all his shit
Drained him of blood and water

Jesus Christ
It was so sweet

The crucifix reeled over
Not supporting my vampiric girth

I had eaten every last piece
Loincloth and all

Thorns stuck in my teeth

My stomach rumbled,
"I forgive you, my son."

I belched a mighty belch
"What's done, is done."

I woke cold and shivering
Needle hanging out my arm

I curled fetal and quivering
How could I imagine such harm

My stomach again,

"Kill the man,
Be a god."

It Ain't the Wand

It ain't the wand
It's the wizard

It is the gall
Of the man

It ain't no gun or no bullet
But the hate a-raging' in one's hand

Can't be the fire or the acid
That leads the flesh to burn

It's the fury and the passion
Of a soul mid-churn

It ain't no quest or no journey
It's the faith in the soles of the feet

That tread the path
That walk the beat

That love rakin' your heart
The wind a-pullin' your hair

It ain't what you continue to carry
But that you continue to care

Party Girls Feel Nothing

Party girls feel nothing
Because they've all been drugged

Just passed out nude slumped and vulnerable
on vomit, stained rugs

Party girls feel nothing
Because of what hides in their drinks

It's so very hard to feel
When you can't even think

All the roofies and mickies so perfectly
mixed

Leave them blacked out and naked

Leaves them passive and transfixed

Party girls are only party girls
Until the morning comes

Then the women they are
Return to their homes

Return to their families with broken hopes
And terrified moans

They cry in the shower

They cry to their friends

They cry out to high powers

The crying never stops

They warn the young girls

Tell them of monsters and fiends

But no one seems to listen
The monsters are free to prowl
And the party never ends

VERA

You're dripping in television
The static rolling down you
Puddling around your naked form
It's that strange gray-white mixed with blue

The spray paint on your genitals
Was a silver that shined
Like the kind the tin man wore
Before he realized he would mind

The belt around your neck
The one mom got you last year
You said you didn't like it
And now it's mockingly here

Vera,
I pulled the soggy paper bag off your head
It was soiled, ripped
And alarmingly red

The Xs cut deep in your eyes
How could they do you like that
I can't look at you
I'm sorry I can't

You're hands blistered raw
Your face is so twisted
I close my eyes
Hands under nude bruised arms and legs
Lifted

Vera,
Can you remember when?
When we were starry-eyed carefree kids?
We rode our bikes down the mulberry hill
And left the sickest cool kid trickiest skids
I carry you out to the coroner
The lights are still flashing
My mind goes back to Mulberry Hill

We caught fireflies and bumble bees
We shared secrets, had endless summers
Untamed
Nostalgia brings you back to life,
But reality screams...

It'll never be the same

Vera, oh Vera
American shame

Today I Felt My Menace

Today I felt my menace
While walking down the street
A young woman in front of me
Quickly looked down at her feet
As I walked behind her
Her pace began to change
She moved faster and faster
I wondered, "What is the thing?"
This thing I'd done
To kickstart suspicion
To worry her
Was I so red with inquisition?
As I sauntered behind
A quick look back here and there
Her flashing face so concerned
So full of fear
Oh my menace
I realized as I walked into a wall of brick
My menace was hanging between my legs
My dick

A son of Adam

Is all I need to be

For those around me
To feel fear
To feel less free

Well, She'll Lead 'Em On

Well, she'll
Lead 'em on knock 'em down

She never smiles
She flaunts a frown

With the nightmares
Under the crack in the sky

Nah she don't flinch
See she don't crawl

Yeah, she'll
Make 'em squirm
Give 'em hell

An antique kind of attitude
A bullwhip wearing a deep shade of red

She knows the words
She knows what's been said

Draped in silver screen
Lips never wet

She has an ace up her sleeve
She always places a bet

When the book ends with bookends
She's the bitch

She's the salt of the earth
And bloody spit

When the fire dies down to death
She's the next match lit

No matter where she goes
There she

Lead 'em on
Knock 'em down

She don't smile
She confounds

Black-Ringed Eye

Black-ringed eye
Blue slicked shining skin

A man whose been asked twice
And the physical evidence of sin

Hard talks
About harder hands

High waters and awkward navigations
The kind a bruise demands

An obvious evil
With an obvious fix

But this ain't a house of hay
It's a house of bricks

The mortar is stubborn
Despite all its cracks

The walls stand tall
In the face of facts

It might weather the storm
Stand after the fire

But a house can't be a home
When it's slap full of ire

If you've ever seen a demolition
Building vs. ball

You have the understanding
Under violence even the strongest buildings fall

Gone Is the Cash

Gone is the cash
The man in black

Dead be the king
Died in his shit

The purple rain is dried up
It ain't e'er more to sing

The heroes of the day
Live out on Mars

All the deaths the Duke died
On the silver screen were true

All these dudes
They are my dad

They exist in a dream
And it hurts so damn bad

Macho men
The cream

Cream of the crop

All dead and gone
All rose to the top

Pugilist

Woman
You ain't born to man

You was born to know
Things a man can't

The moon follows
You through the months
And so the years

But it's man that fills your heart
With feelin' and fear

So who's gunna love you?
Who's gunna be with you?

Oh, if you're all alone
Can't be told by other women
Lord not a man

Who you're gunna be
Who's gunna be you

No sigh of earth
No shadow of moon

No rising tide
No whining croon

Is gunna pull you
Around

You gotta lotta influence
Weighing down on you

Gravity is a law
Of the universe

All things

Bend to its call

But not you, woman
Skinned
But alive

Free from all things
No laws
Oh, damn the rules

The moon follows you
Woman

Whereabouts will you lead?

'Cuz right now you're flyin'
N' no god or king knows where

You're gunna land

Wallop Festival Scarecrow

A supposin' ease of violence
Has far from any place to hide
Bruised arms and memories
We thought safely left behind
O Lord, why do we hurt
The ones that we done hit
With closed minds n' closed hands
Covered in that warm lacquer n' grist
Yellowed purple blue
Parts of our meat
Goose-egged and aching
Wrapped in torn shirts, bed sheets
Ifin' we were scarecrows
We'd just stuff it back on in
The straw n' hay that is
Not all this slickly flesh
Ifin' only we was old flannels n' stuffing
N' not hearts a-beatin' beneath breasts

Body Grapple Shindig

Fixin' to crack

Knuckles
Necks
Or spines

Unspecified in order
Anthropomorphic in kind

Flexin' and pullin'
A far sight from fine

Muscles strainin'
Taxed to rippin'

Fibers torn and tearin'
Unionized for violence

An army of cells
Ionized in aims of dislocation

Splittin' fingernails bitin'
Chewin' for leverage

An evolutionary art of anger
Preformed out right au natural

Welcome to the ball
Buckaroo

You leadin' the dance
Or the dance leadin' you?

Grab hold n' boogie

Jazz Hands

Jazz jazzy jazz hands
Flamboyant burning jazz hands

Shake 'em 'til they bleed
Shake 'em hard as you can

Shake those shaky fucking fuckers right the
Fuck off

Shake 'em 'til they happy
Shake 'em 'til they quiet

Shake those fucking hands

Shake 'em for me baby
Shake 'em like an autistic child

Shake those goddamn hands

Shake 'em like a baby
Shake 'em like a screaming child

SHAKE Those goddamn jazzy jazz bleeding
jazz goddam hands

SHAKE

Don't Make Us Jam You Up

Run for the door old-head
We ain't need you round here no more

You been out a elbow grease
That much is clear

Bad knees n' weak fingers
Thinning hair

You headed for the cooling board
N' that ain't a bet, it's a steal

A real cut-fence kinda cat
Maybe twenty years ago

But this is new blood in the river
N' buddy you just don't swim

Second class is a bit much
'Cuz you a damn sight past ain't

Don't call it backlash
This just some down the pipe news

If you couldn't see it comin'
Well that just proves the point

We ain't here to take you home
Just to show you the door

We ain't your family
Never was
Old timer
Don't make us

Acceptable Losses

The varnish of life
Has only as much gloss
And as much shine

As the hand applies

More
Or less

It depends
On the eyes

Shimmer
Glimmer
Glisten
Gloss

How much is life?
How much is loss?

I Loved You in the Morning

They pulled the stars off this flag
Sewed 'em to their foreheads

They know where we sleep
'Cuz its right next door

Well, I'd says it's more than frightening
Seein' how they know they're so right

You can hear the spit hit the floor
In between the shouts and caterwauls

Pointing fingers
Slammin' doors

All the

Ghosts

In the silence before
The sharp inhales
And pained grimaces

They've got it in the bag
All the means and ends

Idolatry in automatism
A far cry

From what used to be
Called patriotism

Folks died for this
That's what they'll always say

Can't help but wonder
If all them dead folks
Would want things this way

Displacement

Deep dark basement
Sioux Falls South Dakota

Stroked out
Foam mouth

Rat shit in the corners
Bat shit in the brains

If everything is different
Everything doesn't include chains

The rat bat is on the wall
Mounted and scarred

Covered in blood
Guts and gore

A weapon of mass destruction
Generations by the score

Etched and tallied
Grip to tip

The snow drifts in from the window
The sink and pipes leak a steady drip

The folding chair is busted
But I sit just fine

All these things are horrid
But they are still mine

I could fix them yes
This is true

But throwing all these stars back
Feels like to much to do

Perfect midwestern night
A sky dressed full black

No twinkling or shining
That's all and
That's that

Sesame Street Drug Test Blues

She took me way on over
Threw the clouds down the way

The sun's mocking me
Unequivocally in sway

There's another bastard at the door
I can smell him from here

I don't have the guts to face him
I can't dance another, dear

It's been too long and too much
These holes are too big

I've eaten so many bottles
I've seen so many spins

All these liquids
In my guilty piss

A sweet request I make in the morning
Please don't jam me up

I'll be outta work
I just need to fill that cup

My side is not abreast
Yeah be alone

I've run my boon companions
With a holler and a moan

I have no man standing
I canny be heard

No Kermit No Grover
No Snuffleupagus
No Big Bird

Jazz on the radio
Jazz them hands

Bring on the punches

Again.

Positively, aced.

Down in Tijuana

Down in Tijuana
They gather round

A duel drew them in
Gave them the show they expect

One man dead
Another still erect

What a phallic show of prowess
What a spectacular feat of strength

To gank another hombre
Mi hermano

Over some jest

Still the fastest
still the best

They cheer and whistle

But that's nuts to me

A dead man in the street

Is all

I see

Outlawyers

You can't be punk rock if you're a Nazi
See, thems the rules

Sames as no jaywalkin'
No cussin'
N' no crank ifin' ya wanna be a preacher man

Thems just the rules

It don't matter if they're written or not

No it ain't fascist, it's just the way things are

Wipe that shit off yer face kid
It's nine a.m.

N' if it ain't here
Then it is somewhere

Act like it

No exceptions

Clean on up

Punk.

Twelve Year-Olds Don't Know About Watergate

I've read some manifestos
I've seen some cataclysms

I've heard some prayers
And taken part in cannibalism

So if I can't have serenity
Well, I'll take apocalypse now

Because if God flooded it all once before
I sure hope he's still around

I see no revolt or revolution
Just the earth around the sun

Everything's the same
It begins and then it's done

Just a rock covered with skin

This planet keeps on spinning

A screaming barrel of monkeys

Gnashing and cavorting

So don't call me existential

Or I'll go all America on your ass

Don't tell me that it's greener
When you know there isn't even grass

If I've puked once
Then I've puked a thousand times

If I've written down a word
Then I've written all its rhymes

Those words all ring hollow still
That vomit smells the same

There's eight billion screeching people
But I can only hear their shame

So I hope that floods a comin'
Or that fire rains down from clouds

Because all this compromise is deafening
and So unbearably loud

So if I can't have apocalypse
Well, then I'd rather die

With no false hopes and no apologies
My guns still at my side

It's Hard to Live in the City

It's hard to live in the city

But then

It's hard to live anywhere

With all these opinions and problems

It don't seem like platitudes and sympathy
Gunna cut it

Not anymore

Not with all them fake news
Them there revelations
Them big bad predators

Seems like something else might could do
Though

Seems that thing might could be

Answers

Might could be bullets too

Perchancin' it might not be so hard to live in the City

Or anywhere else for that matter

If the man behind the curtain, the hare, and the Hatter

Would just come out and say what them Sumbitches been up to

Over the last ten or twenty years

Maybe if we stopped using these here wooden Swords to fight these very real dragons

Maybin' it might not be so sumbitchin' hard

To live in the city

Or just about any place else

Might could be

But probably not

It's so goldurn hard Jesus lord

To live in this city

And anyplace

You're Gunna Carry That Weight

You're gunna carry that weight

In your shoulders
On your back

Mostly void

Partially light

The plasma twists
Her pearls clack

The smoke signals
Done stepped out

For a drink

The nightmen done arrived
know who you are

How you think

Oh, yes

You're gunna carry that weight

In your eyes
On your neck

Points of white

Unfurled black

The flame dances
His ace leaves the deck

Later

Cowboy

Collect

Taste

Guns Taste Bad

Guns taste bad
But people still eat them

In the pursuit of happiness, but more often
Freedom

N' folks say afterwards
Down in the lake of fire

Those souls burn
With regret and ire

Well horse shit

What's one swallowed bullet
Or a handful of pills

Compared to a life of force-fed agendas and
Malevolent wills

Leave these suicides alone
They can't hear you anymore

They've left the game
On an unfair score

Don't tell them where they're going
When you can't say for yourself

For all you know
They're kicking sweet flips
And grinding sick rails

At the cosmic skatepark
With every other lonely fetus that ever failed

Featured on YouTube and iFunny
Ripping fat vape mods

Prank clips trending on insta and twitter
Reposted, liked by God

Adam Kadmon and the Folks Who Eat Him

Shoeless
Sores on the feet

Nakedness
To total shame

Hollow words
In hollow men

Slow reaching hands
For bridges burned

Untucked
Sullied

Vertically aligned carbon nanotube arrays

It isn't the absence of light
But the near abject absorption of it

Darker than black esotericism

How's everything tasting?

It tastes just fine.

The Ziggurat of Self Appraisal

As big as you're feelin'
Or maybe as small

A lost temple
In the shape of you

Grandiose
To decrepit

Filled with hidden treasures
Closeted skeletons
Wailing ghosts

A shimmering enclave
In turn an infested vacancy

As many levels
Gilded walls
And cobwebs

As you got

Hanging

Barricading

Or Shining

From without
And within

Hecate

If I could have chosen
To be a better friend

Who would I have been

Maybe Kinder
Or Harsher

For whatever I have been to you
Or whoever else

Crossroads of passing
Between us and myself

I have been inadequate
With all my puppet strings

Misplaced feelings and emotions
Decorations for human beings

Compassion held as a flaw
Pity clutched to sin

Honesty carved as law
Sorrow given where it should have been

I forsake my knowledge
My magic and witchcraft
My plants and ghosts

My
Sorcery
And necromancy

At your borders

Here's to sworn enemies
In this life

And the next

I hand you the torches
I cast out the
Sword

I hand you my keys
So sayeth
The Lord

Diogenes

Here is the heraldry
Tapestries of hard times

Droning in the head
Drones behind clouds

Leaden water
No power to absolve

Faces turn away
Faces don't look at all

Distance grows wider
Bonds stretch only so far

We haven't asked yet
We cannot try

The chemicals
The hormones

Thoughts of freedom
Died with instinct

Bound to the mantel
We build ourselves

In comparison to whom

Virtual competition

Sew us back together
Chickens without feathers

There might be angels in an outfield somewhere
But it ain't here

Behold

Diogenes II: Spittoon

If cleanliness is what them folks 'd say

Then there's a sacrilege in dirty dishes

Heresy in that fouled befouledry

Blasphemy in them soiled implementations

Soz maybe let it be a heretic

Covered in hated filth 'n putrefied sin

To cast a first stone

To them clean glass houses of them clean rich Men

The framing of bacteria

That there slander of disease

Writ by gibbering apes

Who done dang need to believe

Libel passed down doggone millennia

Against old timey entropy

A history of boot lickin' euphemisms

True blue calumny

They say the sun shines on cesspools

N' remains unpolluted

But then, sun's radiant

N' all that hangs on floatin' about it is irradiated

Unclean

The Hand That Offends

I had a tooth
That ached

So I pulled the thing out

It was painful
And excessive

My mouth wouldn't stop bleeding
My shirt stained at the collar

Ruined
A snowy white
Covered in a crimson
Soon
Turned brown

My eyes held my visage
Drunk and freewheeling

In the mirror I swayed

Fixated on the piece of me
Removed

Complete and free
Away from the rest

Losing its feeling
Losing its life

Separate from the whole
Doomed to die

A million cells condemned
By the choice of he
The decider of the body

Bare it not fruit

May it die
Never to be eaten from again

Cast out
The enamel finds a home

With the tissues
And tampons

Trash
Among trash

Obsolete
Destined for the land of decay

Landfill
Dump
Rot

Smashed Thumbs

Well, everyone is there for you
'Til they ain't

'Cuz it's a solitary beat
Livin' a life post truth

Hard to say
If it's worth

Some proud moment
Or a whole lotta bein' right

If that's all you're gunna have to show

Ain't the same

Same as bein' loved

Havin' some sense of shared reality

But ifin' it's only you
Well, now how could you be wrong

Solitude is a solace
Shaped like a hammer

I tell you what

It hits like one too

Plantation Wedding

Impermeable alabaster walls
Inescapable ivory compounds

Structures and institutions
Old and insidious

Violent invisible empires
Seen by many

Ignored and lingering
A silence that calls

We are not in this together
We are separate

We have not made it through worse
We are segregated

We never unified
We have been and remain shattered

We are not we
There is no us

But there is a they
There remains a them

Suffocated by fragility
Dying for agency

So dance upon floors
Stained in their blood

Pose for photos
In the fields of their torment

And laugh with your friends
Where your forefathers did the same

Between alabaster pillars
Inside ivory walls

Practicin' Haptics Physically

Now thinkin' is a whole bowl
Of theory

Lots of ideas
N' lots vibrations

Synapses lightin'
And flashin'

Deep in that fancy gray
Calculator

In the watery meat jelly
In yer fancy white skull

Atoms movin' around
Dancin' the electron shuffle

Sounds like a whole lotta doin'

But it ain't a gotdamn sight

Ain't a finger lifted
Ain't a pat on the back

No hands held
No arms outstretched

Just a heap a wasted energy

Dwellin' ain't never gunna do a thing

That a hand on the shoulder
Or arms round the chest

Done in a million billion years

Thinkin' is done enough to be
Called commonplace

But doin' when the doin's scarce
Is as much as ya can do

Heavyweight Round 12

I am locked in an unending fistfight.

An angry, brutal, and wild brawl.

No matter the fight I put up or the hurt I put out.

Gravity,

Time,

And sleep

Win every single bout.

Fists up,
Come out swinging.

Appaloosa

The brush lays a heavy coat
Black and blinding

The feeling of water
Over lungs
Skin
Spine

Floating

Mind over matter

Bring your head out of that pool

Over the bombs
The politics
The violence
The government
The black paint

Stand in the tub
That shallow bucket

Breathe

That feeling of floating
Gone

Atop your legs
Strong and holding

Again and again

Step back out

From the water to the ground

Free of holding
Free of captivity

Free to walk the earth
Free to feel the wind

Those sounds that once jarred
Now sounds of liberty

No barriers
No holds
No bars

Straddle that horse again
Take the reigns

Ride

Reprieve

Busted teeth
Fat lipped
Lifted words we cannot say

We spit blood on the ground
One another
In wanton dismay

The mitigation is never ending

The simple soliloquy

We cannot reduce this

Survivor's ennui

Saturated
Wrought in forlorn hubris

Tormented
Plagued by this animus

We yearn to be affirmed
Affixed our confessions

Flagellated and yoked
Broken for absolution

So we hoist these sacrifices
We heft that stone axe again

We covet delivery from
These hungers in that we've lain

Loam Sleep

Scrimping for the dawn
Scratching to the moon

With broken wagon wheel stuck deep the fettered muds

The burn scar
Hairless
Numb n' tight

Oxygen deprived
Slogging lost in clay
Bogged

Still muted
Caught silent by hand

There's smoke
But fire here lacks

Just cold ashes
Irradiated graphite
Miasma

Sometimes a moon shadow pop a head into the Door

But not most the time

Hardly not

Anymore

You Creatures

You creatures
You cry

It's subliminal

Within the molten moments
That shift and change

I see a tear

A weakness

An animal weakness

It is perfect and primordial

Raw and uncovered

Flush with alcohol and substance

But true all the same

I envy your truth

You creatures
You created

Cry

Animal Shame

That weighted feeling
In your bladder
In your gut

A whole lotta shit n' piss

Chock full and 'boutta burst

Lines too long
Them shitters full

But the woods is private
Ifin' you know where to go

So stumble on out
Into the dark
The thorns
The burrs

Crouch where the shadows are

Secret shame

If someone sees
You're the toiletry fame

Grab some leaves
Wipe them animal holes

Buckle back that belt

Shamble back to the grounds

Only the possums
N'
The crows saw

Free of shit
Emancipated your urine

Walk tall
Laugh loud

Ain't no one
See your bits
Shits
Or stream

A modern success all the same

I Seen Animals

I seen animals that don't exist
And folks that don't care

Both the same

Here one second gone the next

I just wish the animals would stay

Forget the rest

It Could Have Been Very Well Designed

It could have been
Very well designed
I take that with salt
The salt takes it with tequila

Your rags cannot fool me
I've seen you with your wealth
Those bonds you bear
Are mass produced
Fool's gold

They crack the tooth
They green the neck
Film props
Costume jewelry

You wear it well
Or Maybe it wears you

Either way

You have the attention

An audience

They've bought the whole kit
Kaboodle
Farm
And farce

Adios

Freeloaders

I've been seeing white faces
In the windows

A red stranger by my car

Friends tell me that it's angels
Lo, do not be afraid

But if I've read my scripture right,
That's the line all angels love to say

But the faces do not speak,
The red woman remains mute

The faces watch unmoving
The stranger
She follows suit

So in repose
I do the same

Here and gone
Unknowing who to blame

A banal surveillance
I ignore them
But they do not seem to care

Now joined with hollow sounds
And invisible fingers in my hair

The false explosions echo as I lay restless
The baseless carnival music fades in and out

But when alone in my room
The hand runs down my back
Causes me to shout

God is in the house

A Ball of Mental Illness

A ball of mental illness
Dancing out of time

Much more tequila
Very little lime

Home again

Smiling sycophants
In pastel dress

Sticky notes and atom bombs covered by press

Home again

Scoobs is dead
Scrappy Doo too

Saturday morning
Has bid adieu

Jiggity jig
Gravity is more pretentious and dislikable

Than any other possible singlet of physics or Philosophy

Home again
Home again
Jiggity jig

It'll pull you apart
No matter how big

Corporate Adjacent

Like smoke in the dark most things go unseen

We can (not) commit

Open rebellion

So a trillion minuscule revolts

In twitching eyebrows

Flared nostrils

Grit teeth

Black hats and black flags

We can (not) save

Those in thermopile

From the amassing crowd

In kevlar and plastics

Locked n' loaded

Opinionated

State owned satellites and foreign funding

We can (not) unbind

The place we are born

Now the fingers tear

At locks of hair

To eyes

Skin

If words were so very mighty

They'd outlaw them too

Jargon

Claptrap

Hullabaloo

The Vault Opens

Silver tongues
Clenching teeth

Swearing oaths
Slithering in sheaths

Reparations withheld
Truths long untold

Cards flattened to the chest
High aces bend to the fold

Aching backs
Splintering spines

Twisted and contorted
Behind cold buttoned eyes

Hands of horror
Ragged stained nails

Grasping and scratching
To open books of fabled tales

Clasped tightly by witch words
Bound in shuddering slicked flesh

Grimoires buried deep
In shallow sinking breasts

Old scars and damning markings
Hidden in the shifting murky pond

Revealed and accepted
Unfurled in the howling dawn

Motives loosed in spoken tongue
Or moving hand

Await the verdict,
Be it pardon or be it damned

You Gave Me Acid

You gave me acid
I drank the whole bottle

It wasn't so bad
Didn't take long to swallow

But the next glass you slid my way
Was another thing entirely

It burned all the way down
I can still feel it inside of me

It turns like hook lined worms
Tears the lining of my stomach

You smiled I remember
When I emptied the cup and grimaced

A barkeep from hell
All the demons witnessed

And laughed as I downed your goblet of
Rejection

The twisting shark tooth grins
Etched into my skull

All these ulcers in my gut
Cancers along the intestinal wall

You didn't force me to drink
And I still quaffed it all

Well, I'm Not Sure If I Am Back

Well, I'm not sure if I'm back in Nebraska
Maybe, hell

Either way, I'm lost
So it's not a big deal

A place is a place
And I'm just a thing

Unseasonably warm
Engine's been idling

Heat waves off the pavement
Shake the cars off in the distance

There's werewolves in the cornfield
Coated in sweat

Just more animals
Painting the county roads red

Goddamn clouds
Hide the moon

Hell or high water
Trip is soon through

I Have Killed

I have killed

In dreamscapes and in my mind.

Violently.

The old and young.

I awake ashamed and repulsed

Do I call them nightmares?

I have killed the seed of my mind

I have hacked and slashed and maimed and Twisted

A memory of a dream is still a memory.
Who am I to say what is real and what is not.

If I am so vicious in my dreams,

What can be said of me while I wake?
If I murder a-slumber.

The line between dreams and reality is hidden at dawn

And I wake, as guilty as ever.

A Greasy Spot on the Heart

Innocence is a damning idea

As is guilt

The paradoxical nature of these two dogmas

Has produced
Procured
And proclaimed

Most if not all the great tragedies of humanity these last 5000 years

Or from the time humans developed a sense of Righteousness
Or morality as a form of law

A consciousness

This abject consciousness
Over instinct and intuition

Has led to the mass anxiousness and Dejectedness

That lies deep seated in the recesses of the "Soul" of humanity

The inevitable loss of (illusionary) innocence And the following Wracking grief of guilt
(Of knowing one cannot re-attain the afore mentioned "lost" innocence) leads one not only To feel as if they have "sinned" but also to not Understand as to why

Guilt cannot exist without innocence and so Innocence cannot be defined without guilt

The pair exists solely in the philosophy
Producing extra grey matter and
Superficial synapses which birth that
invisible And indefinable idea which is
consciousness

Below you will find
A written confession of all my crimes

The times and places of the acts

The locations they've been buried

And the names I've prescribed them

I have lived

Signed pretentiously,

Landon J. Chapman

Bad

You've Got a Face with a View

Speak into my mouth
Scream down my throat

Tell me how to be

Be the salt on my lips

Whisper the words to my teeth
Yell an oath around my tongue

Tell me why I'm dwelling

How you got that light in your eyes

Sing into my skull
Whistle past my ears

Tell me again how to lie

Be a semblance of true

Because this gun is for hire
Dancing in the light or dark

You've got a face with a view

Upchucked

Last night I threw up
Missed the toilet
Oh well

Nobody here
To worry
About the smell

I tried to walk out back
Ran into the screen door
In the kitchen

My ears rang
My hands were
Twitching

All of the stupid things
I've been
Through

Screen doors
Fights
You

Maybe I did the wrong thing
Maybe I should have
Stayed

Maybe your mind
Might have
Changed

No

I wipe the blood off my nose
And the vomit off
My mouth

Stained sleeves

Beer barf
Under the Milky Way
Somewhere
In the south

She's So Tall

She's the lead
This time

'Cuz this ain't a dance for feet

But he's following her motions
Anyhow

So long
So neat

The way she's holding him
His head on her shoulder
Well that's a waltz he's never seen

There is no soundtrack playing
Her hand on his back
No music for the scene

She's mouthing softly
Down into his ear

So softly
So gently

He almost can't hear

She's so tall

That when he looks
Up at her

In her white heels
And mascara

He realizes

He can't see it running
Until it's down past her chin

You Were a Library

Full of all my favorite books,
Photo albums, VHSes,

Kind hearted looks

And I had a borrower's card
With no limit

No holds
No bars

And I read every book I could
Watched as many decks
Looked at all your looks

Kept a few past date

But now the shelves
They're barren

No books

No photo albums

Just cobwebs
N' dust

If it's all the same

The same
At least to you

I'm a-gunna hold on
To the few that I'd kept
Past Date

Over-due

When You Were Leaving

Black jacket

Bold

And steely

Those zippers
Were broken
Just How you preferred them

N' that's unspoken

But I'll never hear you tell
Me

How

Like anything between
Us

Someone is Christ

And someone's
Judas

But that'll stay

Buried

With the Polaroids
And Bookmarks

Now

I've been
Trying

So I'm still
Lying

Lightly and
Dearly

Darkly and
Clearly

Promises
I cannot keep

Crocodile tears
I refuse to weep

So leathery

So steely

Bold and broken

Now

Doubt

If it's not how much you love but how hard you Try

And god made dirt and dirt don't hurt

Dirt don't try

And it sure don't die

Is it worth it?

If it's a hammer to the face
Or knife to the gut

I see your face
So I see the face of God

Eyes closed
A mouth sewn shut

You love unconditional
Vast and far

But it's the trying that matters
And in that you've been

Subpar

Thanks Mom

Thanks mom
Thanks dad

I'm here now
With genes and cells

Speckled with mutations
Some tics and tells

Not great at poker
But I can play the game

Dealt a raw hand?
You just hide your shame

But that's not very fashionable
To the propagandist's point

The Times
The Post
The Blaze
All share the same agenda every night

Everyone's supposed to be a pirouetting dancer

Regardless of trifling issues
Like overpopulation, famine or cancer

Just spin with the slow melody of the shiny Sousaphone

Step to the click of the punch clock's Metronome

Stay in rhythm
Watch your feet

Don't step on any toes

Or bruise anyone's meat

So thanks again

I've got all of evolution behind me
Some real intelligent design

Humming the same syncopated melody
Playing the cards as divined

Long Distance Tokyo

It's three a.m.
You call again

The stones gather in my chest and
I'm terrified

I don't know what to say
So I just beg you not to jump

When you ask why not

I lie

I say because I'd never do that to you

Then the tears come through the telephone

And I'm horrified because I think you know
the Truth

So I stutter and I stall just to keep you on the
Phone

But the line goes dead
Then you don't answer when I call

Thomas and I
Just wide awake

Wondering

Hoping

For a call from you

And not some Japanese coroner

It's ten a.m. in Iowa
The phone rings

Hello?

It's Nice You're So Happy

I'm glad

Wish I could know you better

But you're somewhere else

Past the thousand yard stare

Round the bend

You smile

Your glasses flash

I'm in the reflection

Big eyes empty

Hands the same

You're doin' fine
On the outside

Anyway

Come Back Soon

Come back soon

It'd be so good to see you

Come back soon

We've had to learn to bid adieu

There's plenty to talk about
But you've been so far away

Hurt to see you go
Had so much to say

Maybe next time
We won't be so small

Hard to reach this distance
Harder to say it all

Do you even sound the same?
Wish we could see all that's changed

Hope you've been doing well
Can't help but feel estranged

Come back soon

Can't wait to see you

Come back soon

We've all learned to miss you

I'm not sure
If you'd remember

How things used to be

Not sure I do either

We'll never know
Not in good faith

Who we'd be
Without all this space

Comeback soon

Comeback soon

It'd be so nice

To see you.

The Hardest Thing About Being a Broken Family

The hardest part of being a broken family

Is coming back together

The pain of seeing one another

Of weathering
The only weather

That brokenness allows

To gather
Together

In times of joy

For the broken family

Will forever be tainted with a tear in the eyes

Sweet melancholy reunion

Sweet bitter cries

The burden of a broken family

Is that the family still tries

Bonghwang

Changed hands that reach out
To backs turned in self affirming scorn

A face shaved
Shedding the past

Smiling longingly
Proudly
Tearfully

Across the expanse of estrangement and
Excommunication

Swarmed and covered
In self-inflicted and indicted
Scars of guilt

Rebirth is impossible
Clean slates are a lie

Redemption is only
For those baptized by fire

I've Seen You in the Wind

I've seen you in the wind and in the trees
On a cliff face and in my dreams

You're happy you're gone but I'm here alone
Now I'm nobody's son

With flowers in your hair
And a song on your tongue

These teeth in my mouth coated in hateful Breath
Cursing god for his graces and mercies

Damn this man
I puke up my secrets my guts

Demons made of ulcers,
And angry blood clots

Those flowers grow thorns
About your eyes, now great green horns

Drying and dying the flowers peel away
Leaving the smiling skull of a skeleton to stay

The song is quiet and soft as your tongue fades To black
Soon I'm gripping at just ashes to have you Back

Headlights Out

Headlights Out
Dead lights for the trash
Old electrical rubbish?
Thrown out.
Smash.

Lost child
Soul taken by the wicked
Worn out. Worn in?
Strung out.
Junky.

Match burnt
Struck
Char forgotten wood?
Waiting for her friend.
Ash.

Convicted felon
Branded
Untouchable, unlovable?
Vile.
Pretend.

Abandoned shack
Sagging and empty
Mildewed. Infestation?
Fuel.
Arson.

Hope
Remade and shining
Feel the feeling?
Recycle.
You must be dreaming.

Shame Rain On Me

Give me all your

All your dissatisfaction

All your sleepless nights

Pain rain on me
Give me all your

All your unheard cries

All the black dresses

As I stare into the mirror
With your horns on my head

That hate saw empathy
That pain blossomed flowers

These horns grew wings
Free as a bird

Born from ashes
In an old coffee cup

I saw god fly away
As the sky opened up

Evil rain on me
Give me all

All your world

All the tears
All the silence

As I return to the mirror
My fears now sweet

I burn to nothing
And soar from the cup

Medusa

Stone man
And snakes

Old timey religion
For the faux and fake

Liars and philanderers
A cold sliver in the night

Regalia and ritual
Embers of sacred signs, cool in the ground

Yours is the silver tongue
The poodle skirt
The letter jacket
The hokey pokey

Yours is the dance hall

Twist

Cavort

Oh Medusa

Consort

It's last call

Yours is the man of constant sorrow

Yours is government work and
Work for Christ

Stone man
And snakes

You are my sunshine
My only sunshine

You know the rest

Slipping Tongues

Slipping tongues
Counting teeth

Telling lies
Slithering secrets

To each other
To the ground

Arched backs
And sweating spines

Thrust to the night
The trillion shining eyes

Hands of horror
Ragged stained nails

Grasping and digging
Telling those tallest tales

To those that will listen
To the whispering air

Old scars and damning markings
Hidden in the shifting moon shadow

Revealed and accepted
Unfurled in the howling dawn

Imperfect
Gorgeous

Two planets
Misaligned

The Soviet Moonshine

Snakes down my throat

Around my spine

I count your teeth
And you count mine

If this is hedonism
I guess I don't mind

Cold hands clasping

Shamelessly intertwined

Your breath is wind
My ears confine

Your father disapproves
And so did I

But this communist bootleg
Has changed my mind

So the moon rises
Your eyes a full eclipse

The sleet and rain
Melt between lips

A kind of Russian depression

Bitter
Never sweet

Passed from mouth to mouth
A taste of chewed and spoiled meat

This is how I'll remember you
How you'll remember me

Washed in Soviet depression
Alone and together

We collapse
We concede

Obduracy

I was wrong
To begin with

You probably knew
Isn't that half the fun

Galaxies apart
In sight and sound

Surprising to say
Again then
You aren't around

As far as
I could tell

Anyhow
I'd say
Or tell myself
You're better off

On that side of space

In a different car
On track another race

I was wrong to begin this

This party
This sin

But you knew that to begin with
At least that's how you'd act

Out in the sun

With a hand on your hip
Your dad behind you

Arms always crossed

I was wrong to begin with
But you could have said something

How are the stars
The planets
Over there?

I'm sure
At least

Gravity's the same.

The Hole in the Pipe Your Ex Gave You

God.

God will demand you move on.

In unfettered debts.

In violence.

In burnt out holes.

Will you pay those dues?

Will you strike those close?

Will you crush that sorry charred briar?

Even if you don't,

Even if you can't,

Things done changed.

Nairobi 98

Lungs fill with dust
Shoulder blades rearing
Rubble slides off back

Palms press hard on hot gravel
Twisted metal
Arms collapse

Eyes closed tight
Open to heat and smoke
Legs ache under the rack

Lay back into the heat
Lightheaded and warm
Sirens sound, fire cracks

Slicked and tired
Heart beating slow
Eyes close to black

Your Sunflower Dress

It was black
It was yellow

It was watchin' me
'Cuz I was watchin' you

When you threw your bags
Then yourself

 Down the stairwell

You put a big hole in the wall

Your bags opened up

Spilled out all my favorite things you wear
Bits of plaster in your hair

But your sunflower dress
It was ruffled
It was wrinkled

Had its eyes all trained on you

'Cuz you were cryin'
And then laughin'

I was laughin' too

We didn't go to your mom's

You slept the day away

You swore that you were fine

I picked up all your clothes
All Your patterned socks and t-shirt bras

And your sunflower dress too

It was sad
And bruised

It was watchin' me

And I was watchin' you

The Factory Is Closing

The factory is closing
The smokes light up

The windmills flashing
Red lights far away

Pitch black January Morning
Nobody speaks

No sun
No moon

In the frozen plains
Nothing moves
Nothing creeps

The void hangs soundless
Speckled with light

Orion is silent
The Dippers are mute

But the lights in the sky are stars

And I swear I can hear them sing

Boober in the Land of Ferrofluid

I was asleep
And I saw vast silent creation

Only to eke to a world
Wherein everything screamed

A horrid arithmetic rises within me
An insidious plague of logic

Compiled and completed
Add nauseam

This cold magnetic waking world
Is filled
Yes
With life

But they are a gnashing and guileful wyrm

Honest
Terrible
Screaming

The wyrms are everywhere
In everything
Coiling and cavorting

Here
That place where even gravity shrieks

So I cannot return to that silent land

Now that I too
Would scream

Blue Little Bell

It is raining
Hard and harsher
Than you have ever known

I hope that you're dry
And warm
But I know that you are not

There is great violence
And aggression
More than you have ever seen

I hope that you're safe
And unharmed
But I know that you are not

You are alone
You are hungry
Scared
Wet
Abandoned

You are all I can think of

The sky is flashing
Brightly and louder
Than you could ever dream

I hope that you're not scared
Not terrified
But I know that you are

Damn this rain
Damn this thunder
Damn my eyes and my ears
Goddamn it all

If I could just hear

You

You're meowing
Or your blue little bell

It is a deluge
Loud and violent

Damn this rain

Metatron

The whole of the human psyche

Is a beloved dead dog

A friend we made

In mirror

Then dashed to the ground

They say a dog will place a paw upon you

In a way to show its love

And so we hold it hoping

That we can do so in turn

But we cannot

We resent bitterly the bonds we form

With those better than ourselves

The comparison of gods n' men

Is a tale as old as time

Pure things of purpose and loyalty

How could we ever chance this gap

How could a simple animal

Be as to the hands that mold the clay

The whole of human despair

Is a dead beloved dog

Long in tooth

Typically blind and tinged with gray

But dead

All the same

A name like his master

ABOUT THE AUTHOR

Landon Chapman grew up in a northern town and currently lives in the deep south where he longs for a taste of cold winters and golden summers. Chapman is a prolific poet who enjoys pipe smoking, drinking and speaking more than his fair share. He is currently working on his first novel.

Thank you for buying a Mango Jane Book
from the Inspired Mind Literary Series.
If you would like to bulk order this book,
please contact the publisher at:

MANGOJANE.CO

www.ingramcontent.com/pod-product-compliance
Lightning Source LLC
Chambersburg PA
CBHW051829160426
43209CB00006B/1093